Illustrations: Mary Beth O'Connor

Author Photo: Virginia A. Miller

Yellow Sofa Press
Brooktondale, NY

ISBN 9 781087 816937

# Acknowledgements

In a Farm Kitchen—1940, *The Healing Muse*, *Before We Knew* (Foothills Publishing)
Cheese, *A Network for Grateful Living* (Gratefulness.org)
Wherever You Are, *The Healing Muse*
Front Porch, *Before We Knew* (Foothills Publishing)
The Artichoke, *A Network for Grateful Living* (Gratefulness.org)
Was That the Last of Buffalo? *Before We Knew* (Foothills Publishing)
Ann's Poem, *The Comstock Review*
Speculation, *Hospicare Newsletter*
Missing, *Hospicare Newsletter*
Meals of Memories, *The Healing Muse*

# Food for Thought

Poems

by

Joyce Holmes McAllister

Illustrated by Mary Beth O'Connor

This book is dedicated with love to Jeremy Webb and Carrie Webb VanGorder, who both know how to cook with flair and savor good food.

# Contents

In a Farm Kitchen

We met eating corn on the cob,
dripping with butter, in a farm
kitchen in 1940. You were eight
and I was nine.

Just outside, scarlet-red tomatoes
hung heavy on the vine, waiting
for some grains of salt. Cucumbers
hid under sprawling leaves, crisp
inside with knobby skins, while
raw green beans snapped against
the tooth, and deep red radishes
stung the tongue.

When you were done with life
for good, you left in mid-season,
the harvest only half-finished;
weeks of ripe corn still uneaten,
the garden laden, waiting.

Asparagus

Why is there such a terrible fuss
about the stalk asparagus?
Some seem to feel
that one must peel
before submerging in the pot,
while others say, "That's tommyrot."

Says Julia Child, the cook's mistake
is drastic if they snap and break
the tough stalk end
and does contend
the whole length will be sweet and tender
if peeled—although a bit more slender.

Now Mr. Beard, our dear departed,
has left a legacy uncharted.
If thin or thick
he says the trick
is peeling when it seems most proper
and, if you must, why then you "chopper."

That gallant southern gent, Claiborne,
who wrote advice from night to morn,
says, "Cut the spear
quite near the rear,
then peel the stalk from top to bottom
abolishing the toughness problem."

So, here I sit with my ordeal,
to snap the end, or do I peel
my wondrous
asparagus?
Ah! Culinary expertise
can leave me clearly ill at ease.

Three

Three times she asked him:
What would you like to eat?
He sat there in his seat
buried behind the news
(silent as her muse).

Three times she longed for a reply,
her patience growing thin.
She walked beyond the door—
met the day, took a breath, flew away.

Three times he called her back—
she left, took a job, became a hack;
she wrote the news he would read,
filled with blood and human greed.

Three times the fantasy grew cold,
the dinner came—
the plates were warm—
the food was hot—
they quelled the storm.

At the Table

The vagaries of man and food
cause me to smile or sometimes brood.
For some, a stint before the table
is one long slurp to make them able
to keep their hunger pangs at bay
and nourish bone and weakened clay.
Their spoon is raised, the head bends low,
as though attacking deadly foe;
the mouth expands without forethought,
the food is swallowed and forgot.
They eat their meal without gustation
not to mention—conversation.

Then there are those who sit for hours
discussing food and all its powers.
Haute cuisine is life and death—
it sparks their blood and gives them breath!
Each flavored, nuanced, subtle smell
unleashes passion, casts its spell.
They savor tastes upon the tongue,
discuss from where the flavor sprung.
Their lives are made, some say defined,
by what they ate and where they dined.
They never heard the term "fast food";
if so, their minds would come unglued.

So as I sit and sup my gruel
I ponder which is bigger fool.

Mr. Goldberg and the Clam

Mr. Goldberg sat and thought
about the clam and what it ought
to do to be more sociable
and therefore more approachable.

He knew if clam would spread a bit
that it would be a fine tidbit.
Since clam knives were so hard to use
he thought he might try charm and schmooze.

"Oh little clam, just open wide
and view the lovely world outside,
the universe of sky and air,
the wonders of the here and there."

But clam was silent and stayed well
within the safety of his shell.
He feared that if he spread a crack
he might end up as Goldberg's snack.

Now Mr. Goldberg told the clam,
"You think because I am a man
that I will rush you down my hatch—
that I would eat you with dispatch."

The clam from deep within his shell
thought, Goldberg sir, I hear you well;
if you should dip me in hot sauce
then I would end a total loss,

and buried deep in your inside,
for me, a clam-like suicide!
Then Mr. Goldberg tried a tack
that was, somewhat, based on fact.

He said, "Dear clam, I am a Jew,
and therefore I cannot eat you.
My mother raised me orthodox!
My conscience says I must eat lox!"

The clam was silent, deep in thought,
as clams will do when tense and taut.
He wondered, What is orthodox?
Were such things truth or paradox?

Now Goldberg, no psychologist,
nor well-informed biologist,
explained, "My mother taught me well,
I cannot eat food from a shell.

Since you have neither scale nor fin
you are a dietary sin;
so have no fear, my clammy friend,
I do not wish to bring your end."

Poor clam began to acquiesce,
which was unwise, I must confess.
He thought Goldberg was quite a gent,
that what he said was what he meant.

So clam, who was a littleneck,
said to himself, Oh! What the heck!
This guy sounds nice and quite sincere,
so I will spread apart and peer.

And then clam opened up his shell
to look at Goldberg long and well,
and ended up a Clam Casino
unknown in Vegas or in Reno.

Cooking For The Lost Generation

Alice B. Toklas
once lived in Paris
with Gertrude, her true paramour.
When the exiles arrived
she escaped to the kitchen
for they often could
utterly bore.

Pablo Picasso
might dine with Stein
and discuss Cubist invention,
while Alice created
a sauce or soufflé
which saved her a critic's
pretension.

When Hemingway supped
with the ponderous Stein
and talked of lovers and war,
Alice B. Toklas
invented a meal
to silence his chauvinist lore.

If F. Scott Fitzgerald
would feign conversation
while drunk on an excess of gin,
Alice B. Toklas
would fashion a feast
to keep them all sane
and sanguine.

When verbose Ezra Pound,
would sit and expound
his array of opinions galore,
Alice B. Toklas
would silence his tongue
with dishes he couldn't ignore.

Alice B. Toklas
would cook in the kitchen
providing her liberation,
from all of the strain
of the guests who were known
as the endlessly
Lost Generation.

Under Pressure

Twelve years old and scared to death,
sitting all alone at our kitchen table, my
eyes glued on the gauge of the pressure
canner as the needle kept slowly climbing,

my eyes burned. I blinked to keep them
opened and focused. I heard again the
warning in my mother's voice just before
she returned to the vegetable garden:

> "Don't let the needle climb above
> fifteen degrees or the canner will
> explode and blow up the kitchen!"

I watched, waited, jiggled the massive
canner off the heat when I got too scared,
and vowed, when I grew up, I would buy
all my canned food from the grocery store.

The Aristocratic Dumpling

The aristocratic dumpling
Is the dumpling that is filled
By a cook of vast experience
Who is dexterous and skilled.

For Italians, ravioli
Is the dumpling of their choice,
It gives meaning to their sculpture
And vibrato to their voice.

The shapely Chinese won ton
Is held in great esteem
If floated in a broth,
Deep fried, or cooked by steam.

And Jews, the whole world over,
Have allegiance as a group,
Sustained by floating kreplach
In every kind of soup.

The Polish love pierogi
And many people claim,
Their consuming helped to foster
Paderewski's fame!

The aristocratic dumpling
Will forever be adored,
For the filling in their centers
Is where the flavor's stored.

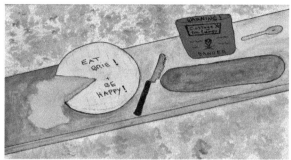

Cheese

Whenever I feel ill at ease
I gain great solace eating cheese.
Its flavor, either mild or sharp,
revives the soul and mends the heart.

A slice of Swiss upon my plate,
with holes to sit and contemplate,
can stimulate my intellect
and make me feel less circumspect.

A cheddar, with a sharpened taste,
may raise sat-fat and thicken waist,
but it can make me feel most fit
when warmed with beer and called rarebit.

A heated brie may help control
the dark malaise within my soul—
but I make sure it comes from France
to never leave the cure to chance.

To find my way as artisan
I may partake of parmesan;
if grated or cut in a sliver,
my muse responds and I deliver.

But not until I reach my dotage
will I ingest the cheese called cottage!

## The Stew

A stew can prove a soggy mess
to serve a friend or any guest.
If cooked without exact precision
it can be met with great derision;
the meat may boil to pallid grey
and have the taste of softened clay,
the vegetables reduced to mush
can cause the cook to curse and blush,
while seasonings, if maladjusted,
will leave the diner quite disgusted.
So if you dare to serve a stew
first ply your guest with hearty brew,
for if your stew is second best
then serve it to a "half-stewed" guest.

Corn On The Cob

Better than money in the till
Better than sirloin on the grill
Better than vodka's "Kettle One"
Better than telling Trump "you're done"
Is corn you eat, fresh on the cob
Now that's as close as you'll get to God!

Wherever You Are

Do they have macaroni and cheese,
the kind you like, top crust
a deep gold, a little crisp, and
underneath, the macaroni
firm but soft to the bite,
the taste of sharp cheese
melted on your tongue?

And hot dogs, Hebrew National,
religiously safe, Jewish mother fattening—
are they marching around together
almost naked, rolls askew, relish dripping,
mustard sliding down their middles,
miniature yellow rivers on the run?
And do you eat one, sometimes two,
like you used to do?

Does someone cook potato pancakes,
and do they make a batch for you,
sputtering in the skillet, ragged edges
curling brown, potato, onion, matzo meal;
do you eat them, every one, hot and
topped with applesauce or sour cream
and then lie restless all night long
from indigestion, latke dreams?

Today I curled my mind around the taste
of early corn and waited for your call,
forgetting it would never come again:
"How do you cook corn on the cob?"
Maybe I should holler into space,
"Not in a microwave—on the stove,
boiling water, five minutes, like every year."
Can you hear me, wherever you are?

The Oyster

Hinged inside a roughened shell
awaiting epicurean whim
poor bivalve, briny, cold, and raw,
defenseless, without tooth or claw,
your future seems both short and grim.

But the gourmand, filled to the brim,
with you and others of your kind
may know a darker side of fate
when belly bloated, filled with ache,
regrets it was on you he dined.

Though you bivalve, can never smile
revenge is sweet after a while!

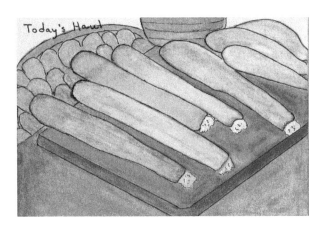

Zucchini

I said to my spouse as he sat
with his paper and ice-cold martini,
"Help me find a new way to prepare
our prolific prodigious zucchini!

"We have ingested this squash lightly grilled,
at times we have eaten it baked—
it once was served steamed and often sautéed
and even made into a cake.

"We have fed on the species for weeks,
and I feel there must be a genie
who produces the gourd overnight
and not one of them grows teeny-weeny!

"I am desperate to know what to do
to get rid of our over-supply."
My spouse's advice, as he added more ice
To his drink so exquisitely dry:

"Cook half of the haul in a soup,
make the rest into sauce for linguine,
Then sit in our garden and vow
We will never again plant zucchini!"

17

## Eggplant Mystery

Despite its name, it's never been
that eggplant grows inside a hen!
Instead, it swells atop the ground
with shape oblong or sometimes round.

It's weird eggplant has such a name.
I wonder who should take the blame?
It's one of species called Nightshade—
did *that* make people so afraid

as to pretend it grew in chickens
so folks would not be scared or sicken
from eggplant grown within the earth
believing in the Nightshade curse?

I don't believe the myth is true.
There is no proof, barely a clue!
Let this strange fruit grow from the soil
and let black earth provide its foil!

(Still, cooking a la parmesan,
the eggplant can cause me alarm.
Can it be deadly? This I wonder
because its kin is belladonna.)

Fondue

The Sixties had a claim to fame
and certainly its share of blame.
But most remembered by a few,
is entertaining with fondue.

It was thought suave and worldly-wise
to serve fondue in any guise,
from melted cheese with crusty bread
to chocolate sauce with fruit, instead.

For those who had guests in to dine,
the fondue pot was made to shine.
It claimed a place on table center
awaiting chef or the presenter.

The fondue forks would reach and stab,
Then folks would know their bite was bagged,
and endless food was then "fondued"
which would be praised and ballyhooed.

But dining fads may grow passé
like manners from another day—
and fondue now may be forgot,
it is well known, we still have "pot."

Front Porch
      T G I F

Sitting on the front porch, chair tilted back,
feet against the rail, you'd wave them in,
friends, acquaintances, old drinking buddies.

They'd drive past slowly on Friday, after work,
check out their welcome. You'd open the door.
Ice cubes would loosen, drop in a bucket,

lemon rinds curl into twists, green olives
drain and wait, ice cubes rattle the shaker,
martinis flow, crackers pile in a basket,

slices of cheese lounge on a plate,
potato chips fall from a crinkled bag,
near a bowl of onion dip, a chunk of ham…

Pickle, onion, mayonnaise spread out
on round pieces of rye. Conversation
floats through dusk, then descending dark.

Someone starts the music, Benny's trio,
Miss Peggy Lee, Ella's scat. Ice melts down
as we melt down. Someone starts to dance.

We watch the college couple next door
make love, shades open, lights ablaze,
sheets thrown off in the heat of passion.

The hour hangs low; only crumbs, crumpled
napkins, a gin bottle tilted against the railing
remain. Our door closes softly, motors start,

pull away. We hurry, dump dishes in the sink,
fill ice cube trays, prepare for bed, remember
the college couple on fire, turn out the lights.

After Forty Years

Sunday afternoons she reads
The New York Times. From his chair,
he watches yard lines, or flips his wrist
to channel in a 50's Hitchcock flick.

Sometimes she peers out briefly,
"Good show at Circle in the Square,
perhaps I'll hop the bus and go." He bends
forward slowly, eyes glued to screen.

February light fades, shadows move
across old snow and up the street,
headed for their night's retreat.
Then a shout, "He got it, by damn, he got it!"

She sighs, puts down the Book Review, eyes him
over lowered glasses, strains to scan his face.
"Are you hungry?" Silence, and then, "I don't know."
She checks her watch, rises, moves to him,

leans across his chest, bumps her nose to his,
heads to heat the stove,
warm Sunday soup, spread garlic butter
over crusty bread, toast it on the grill

until brown ridges form. She pours
some wine, lifts her glass, takes a sip,
thinks about their Sunday afternoons
forty years ago.

The Tomato

The tomato arouses my senses,
no matter what size or hue,
I use the ripe plum
when I wish to succumb
to making a perfect ragù.

The beefsteak is juicy and fat,
its flavor is truly first rate,
when seasoned with basil
and served at the table
on a chilled and well-garnished plate.

The cherry tomato is different—
a tiny round nugget of taste—
when braised with some herb
it is truly superb
and its size can be swallowed with haste!

I adore the bright green tomato,
all floured and then deftly fried,
served up with some bacon—
its joys leave me shaken
but incredibly satisfied.

The tomato inspires all my passion,
sun-dried, in a sauce, or a paste—
it's a grand love affair
with flavor and flair
which leaves me both happy and chaste.

The Artichoke

The artichoke sits on my plate
a vegetable that begs debate.
The novice may but sit and bristle
when asked to eat the ugly thistle.
The uninformed defy all taste
and call the bud an awful waste,
while others, like the connoisseur
or grand gourmand, will all concur
the artichoke of lovely green
is not a veggie to demean.
To scrape the teeth against its leaf
brings utter joy, however brief,
and when one bites into the heart
gastronomy is set apart.
Now as for me and this debate
I find it wise to abdicate.

double serving

bright red lobster on my plate,

how I wish you had a mate—

this greedy one longs to see

two of you just for me!

An Old Question

Debated now and argued then,
"Which came first, the egg or hen?"
Philosophers, psychologists,
and well-renowned biologists
keep up the search and play the sleuth
to find the still-evasive truth.

This question may seem monumental,
and even somewhat transcendental,
to experts searching for a clue—
they sweat and strain and still pursue,
while on this day the egg or hen
could care a whit of such poor men.

The chicken from her hen house perch
doesn't care to do research
of which came first, the egg or hen;
instead she struts about her pen
and clucks, without a single thought
of how she was, at first, begot.

The egg is born without much wit,
and doesn't care to argue it.
It ends up boiled or poached or fried
or grows a chick from deep inside
which may, with time, produce a hen.
OH DEAR! SO HERE WE GO AGAIN!

Child Chef

Long ago, when I was five or six,
And you were old and could no longer cook,
I made myself your chef, to stir and mix
Strange recipes not found in cooking books.
Your widower's cupboards still were overfilled
With flours, sugars, flavors from your past.
I swore, though minus culinary skills,
I'd make a meal for you quite unsurpassed.

I poured from yellowed boxes on your shelves.
Imagination made it all combine.
They turned into a feast for just ourselves,
An old man's meal, unique with my design.

The memory of that meal has fed us long,
Though I am old myself, and you are gone.

Pickled

You are most surely soused and pickled
odd species resting in your brine,
the herring displayed side-by-side
with severed feet from some poor swine.
The sight of you all in a row
incorporate a strange array,
the pearl-size onion, baby corn,
the rind of melon, gone astray.
And now I see before my eyes
the jars of pickled peach and pear,
the egg that once was poached or fried
sits vinegared without a care.
I know that I shall never find
in this array of fickle wonder
a simple item from my youth
I fear it is asunder!
It soaked inside a barrel
and only cost a nickel,
Oh! How my heart would relish now
a dilled and koshered pickle.

Plea to a Pensive Bovine

O solemn cow, well under hung,
who chews her cud with thoughtful tongue,
how well we loved your milk and cream
(we held it in such high esteem)
before its fatty particles
became the cause for articles
that warned us of its clogging power,
leaving us bereft and dour
without whipped cream on pie or cake
unless it was nondairy fake.

Oh solemn cow of endless flow,
who lifts her head when mooing low,
while grazing pastures, munching grain,
remove the fat we all disdain
from bounty held within your udder
so experts will not shrink and shudder,
when butter tops our day-old bread
and once again, we feel well-fed!
Cast off the sin from fat-filled cheese.
but leave its taste to tempt and please.

With well-churned butter, let us braise,
and top our fruit with crème anglaise.
Enjoy our fill of chocolate mousse
while hips and waist constrict, reduce!
Oh solemn cow, with eyes soft brown,
consider how the world would crown
the bovine who removed their guilt
so folk could eat, filled to the hilt,
with creamy richness, savory taste,
and never feel they fell from grace.

Oh solemn cow, act on this thought,
that we may eat and repent naught!

Lament
(Written after consideration of the fact
that summer had come to an end.)

Now I fear has come the hour
when we succumb to cauliflower;
rutabaga, Brussels sprouts,
will feed us now without a doubt.

Turnip smells will fill the house
and may cause some to sigh and grouse,
while mounds of cabbage, cooked or raw,
sustain us through the first spring thaw.

The powerful onion, gentler leek,
will form a sort of winter clique,
while carrots take the center stage
and parsnips follow, unafraid.

Dried beans will soak, then boil or bake,
with every chill and falling flake,
while I, depressed, hold back a sob,
and dream of corn fresh on the cob.

The Turnip

The turnip is maligned by those
who are by nature in the throes,
of constant psychic malcontent—
from which their minds are thus unbent.

The turnip, for the well-adjusted,
and those whose minds are not corrupted,
is just another exploration
in gastronomic toleration.

Cocktail Hour

Before the generation "Beat"
    there was a hour, now obsolete;
  a time once relished, willfully chosen,
      with glasses chilled and ice all frozen,
folks gathered at their favorite grills
  to talk and drink; forgetting ills.

  This time was loud and quite kinetic,
    with ample booze, could end frenetic.
A business might be bought or sold;
     some hot romance could turn ice cold.
  New books were hatched or clothes designed,
  ideas were robbed or undermined.

  This time was known as cocktail hour,
    all filled with gin and rye and power!
The custom ended long ago,
    time alters and refines—
  now, quietly in living rooms,
  folks get as high on wines.

Caviar

How does one speak of caviar?
It is so strange and quite bizarre,
for when removed from world's elite
it is fish eggs the privileged eat.

But ambience can raise the roe
to elegance from status quo.
The serving bowl, to be precise,
should rest in grandeur deep in ice,
while toast points and a lemon wedge
give fish eggs that distinctive edge.

Some minced raw onion, sweetly pungent,
makes caviar much less redundant,
and egg can prove a dandy foil
if it has known a proper boil.

But when the truth is finally told
it's top-shelf vodka, icy cold,
that gives the glitter and the glow
to eggs of fish or sturgeon roe.

Cold vodka in a crystal glass
is what gives caviar its class.

Dinner Out

Sometimes, it really does matter,
can make the difference between
staying or going, forgetting or
keeping old knots in the belly.

You decide to eat out at a really
"posh" place too expensive for
the budget, but worth the price.
to forget, maybe forgive.

You arrive, order drinks, start to
talk, then laugh at some silly
thing neither of you will recall
the next day.

A waiter hovers, suggests the
braised sweetbreads. Sweet
is the feel of the evening,
scent in the air.

He orders tenderloin with béarnaise,
always his choice—so like him.
You share a bottle of Cabernet Sauvignon,
a wine steeped in memories.

Sitting across the table from each other,
candlelight hides wrinkles of time,
but not the years. Now,
you don't ask him for babies any more.

It's far too late. You can still feel his defiance,
fear; your resignation, sorrow.
But tonight is now and real.
You see the outline of his face,

feel his hand touch yours,
wonder if he remembers too.
You know tonight, the only passion
will be a lemon cream soufflé and latte.

You savor it.

He pays the hefty bill, you leave.
There's no desire to rush home,
tear off your clothes,
jump into bed, make love.

He drives the car slowly. You rest your head
on his shoulder, think about next time.
Maybe he will order a different entrée.
You might try their lemon sole.

Toothless

if at a future time my teeth should fail,
fall out, decay to dust, or float away,
i will accept my fate, even prevail
and skirt the perils of a toothless day.
how so, you ask, if such should come to pass?
'cause i remember times when folks made do;
when grandpa gummed his food without a gasp,
forever grateful that old gums could chew.

and then there are false plates, both down and up,
used just for chewing or for vanity,
their nighttime hours spent within a cup,
to help preserve their perfect imagery.

so if in future time i lose them all,
the loss? just faithless loves beyond recall.

The Mushroom

The mushroom grows in numerous guises
for culinary enterprises.
Varieties come big and small
from button to the great puffball,
some, with care, are cultivated
while others, wild, are dehydrated.
The mushroom is devoid of gender
and simply asks to cook in splendor
within a soup or grand pate,
or maybe fired in a flambé.
To flavor a risotto creamy
makes any mushroom simply dreamy;
Oh! never will it feel rebuffed,
but filled with pride, when deftly stuffed.
And when sautéed with wine and butter
the mushroom is set all a flutter.
Though sometimes called a mean fungi,
if poisoned species make folk die,
most mushrooms, gathered wild or bought,
harbor no homicidal thought.

Unpretentious Diner

I.

Sophisticates may eat and drink
in high-class dining places
and never blush or pale or shrink
or get sauce on their faces.

But that, I know, is not for me,
such atmospheres are chilling.
The menus seem a mystery
ambiguous as the billing!

It's "haute cuisine" and "très" gourmet
and menu "á la carte."
I do not parlez-vous français
so I am set apart.

"Prix fixe" is meaningless to me
and so is "carte du jour."
Observers think me bourgeoisie
but never connoisseur.

The waiters all have such panache
they ruin my morale.
I long to ask and not seem brash,
the style of Provençal.

II.

The sternly steward of the wine
is sovereign with decree,
he speaks of vintage, grape, and vine
and makes a wreck of me.

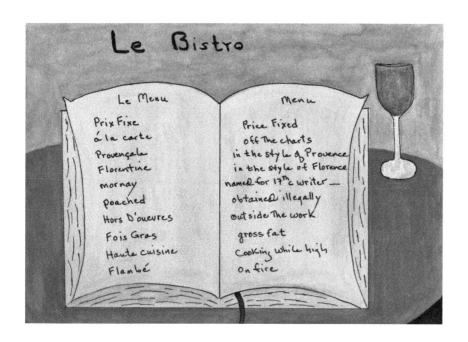

The maître d' ignores my eye,
the bus boy skirts my table.
I think that I am going to die
and wish that I were able!

Garlic

Despite the virtues of garlic
considered by many first-rate,
it can foster disdain
may cause social strain
or alter the course of fate.

Considered by some too lowly
and vulgar for tastes more refined,
others declare,
with a well-knowing air,
all garlic should be enshrined.

Now garlic has virtues aplenty
to defend to the very death,
but its fumes may offend
acquaintance or friend
when lingering upon the breath.

That small pungent clove of garlic,
whose odor is hard to explain,
can break up a party
no matter how "arty,"
if its fumes overpower the brain.

To indulge in the bulb with imprudence
when attending a theater night,
can leave you quite prone
to sitting alone
to ponder the cause of your plight.

Or think of two amorous lovers,
enjoying romantic repose,
when fumes from some garlic
end all of their frolic,
their passion destroyed by the nose.

if breath is heavy with garlic,
but your cooking is truly gourmet,
then cook up a savory
with discretion, but bravery,
and take people's breath away!

Was That the Last of Buffalo?

When that plate fell yesterday,
fragmented like pieces of the past,
was that the last of Buffalo?

The corner grocery store
with cream-filled pastries open
in a cardboard box, long sausages
hung low from hooks above our heads,
and breads, still warm with oven life,
snuggling on their racks.

And in some kitchen,
hidden from our view,
the smell of a ragù rose—
drifted out the door—
and claimed our noses.

We lived in three low rooms
up two long flights of stairs.
Do you remember them?
We sat together, almost touching,
dipping still-warm bread
in garlic-flavored oil
while pasta steamed beneath
a thick red river, and ate at last
those pastries oozing with their
almond custard cream.

I wondered,
when that plate fell yesterday—
"Made in Italy" it said,
deep hollows all around the edge
to hold the deviled eggs—
When the plate fell yesterday
was that the last of Buffalo?
Or did it die with you
so long ago?

I'm sitting in Moosewood, thinking of you

We never came here because I knew
as soon as we entered, your eyes would widen
at the sight of a bar with only eight stools;
perhaps a single male perched at the end,
his pony tail limp, tattoos swirling
up his arms, a single gold earring.

You'd ask, "When did they open this place?"
and I would smile. "Oh! Years ago."
You might agree to be led to a table, where you
would order a double martini—and I would too.
I would study the menu with interest.
You would roll your eyes at me, sigh.

"Only fish, vegetables, beans, rice? Who
dreamed up this menu?" When the martinis arrived,
you'd take a sip and say, "Who's the bartender here?
Must have poured vermouth in a glass and
splashed a little gin"—then mutter, "Doesn't
know an olive from a lemon rind either."

I would offer brightly, "They have very
good salads, and really fine, warm bread,
and did you notice the vegetarian
lasagna with cheese and tofu?" Then
the waiter would arrive to take our
order, and you would ask for the bill.

We would walk past the bar again
where the young man with the tattoos
would wave and say, "Keep well."
We'd head up the street to the usual
place where you would have another
martini, a baked potato with sour cream,
and a thick porterhouse steak.

Ann's Poem

Afterwards we cook, like angels of mercy, determined
to feed our loss. We squeeze lemons dry, make hummus,

cut fruit, full from summer's heat, remove ripened skin
with blinded knives, then watch the severed peelings fall.

We season red tomato, crisp cucumber, hot radish,
with the dry salt of grief. Add parsley, basil, a chiffonade,

one ribbon at a time, like pain we ration, one thought
at a time. Lifeless lamenting robots, we fill empty plates,

demand our tongues to taste again, hoping the flavor
of loss will swallow us into some other space and time

where she sits, pen in hand, blank page filled with words,
intense, shining. We will hear music, her running fingers

touching keys to sound, the notes feeding colored autumn air.
If we cook well enough, carefully avoid the scorch of pain,

season the dish freshly, savor, let life juices dribble down
our chin, she will sit with us, share our table, one more time.

Forgetting

is not easy. I see you spread
butter on the last light
brown remnants of
your pizza crust;

watch you comb your hair
slowly, stray strands
flattened, smoothed in
place with long fingers;

see you even out
the edges of your tie,
fingers deft and swift to
form the knot, pull it tight.

I smile at the careful chef
making scrambled eggs:
low heat, golden fat, long,
slow minutes, careful stirring.

Forgetting is not easy,
but yesterday, and with
no warning, I knew your
birthday had slipped past.

My Funeral Memorial

Most of the people who come
will not know each other;
that may prove awkward—
not for me, but for them.

Some will feel betrayed, for
only after my last warm breath
has cooled, will they realize
they never really knew me.

Some will be certain we are related,
but when the words I have chosen are
read aloud, they will know our
bloods flow in different directions,

mine gushing downhill to the left,
theirs flowing uphill to the right.
In the end, that may not matter.
I was a mystery, anyway, from

the beginning, loving both cows
and words—milking both for all
they were worth, whether under
city lights or in green pastures.

At a point in the celebration, silence
will shelter the room, except for single
voices reading. That will be poets
demanding to be heard. I will be

clapping at a distance, of course.
There will be a piano playing music,
singers and actors I love performing
songs and scenes I have always known.

The most awkward moments will be
eating—a buffet perhaps or lunch.
What will they say to each other,
sitting around, eye-to-eye, fork-to-fork?

I wonder how many times they will
discuss the weather, or the excellent
flavor of the fresh pea soup or crisp
spring greens. I will leave instructions

to serve a very fine wine, and plenty
of it. Last, but hardly least, a bottle
of hearty stout for Margaret. TO HELL
with the gluten for today!

Comfort Food

"Why not eat potato salad on Christmas?
Is there a law?" Then you would describe
tomatoes, picked green in September,
wrapped in newspapers, stored in an
attic until Yuletide when, red like pulp
from the vine, they were ready for eating.

You wanted to greet Noel with corn
on the cob, a thick, juicy steak hot
from charcoal heat. Holiday turkey could
stay stiff in the freezer, or chase a female
through barnyard straw, wild and free
from roasting oven and giblet gravy.

Macaroni salad, a grilled hot dog sealed in
toasted roll, with mustard, relish, running juice,
was a feast worthy of the Savior's birth.
You made that clear, and every year I
waited for your grimace, playing off cabbage,
creamed onions, oyster stuffing, candied yams.

Now, I am refusing summer, leaving the grill
unlit, potatoes raw, eggs uncooked, celery
gritty, scallions whole. I pass by ears of corn,
hear you shout, "Stop, stop!" I answer back,
"I don't want to eat it alone," and walk by.
"Then make potato salad," you whisper.

Your words bring flavors to my tongue.
I think of mayonnaise laced with sweet pickle,
the crunch of green, the soft firmness of spud
and egg. I look up and try to see your face,
feeling a surge of hunger, warmth, happiness.
"Maybe I will," I say, "maybe I will."

Speculation

When you are gone
I will read Maugham again
in this house, like I did
that first summer, turn pages,
gaze at walls.

I may remember how
old plaster begged repair,
the roof kept leaking
patterns on the floor,
money was thin.

I will cook parsnips once again,
coated in brown sugar glaze,
make creamed codfish, let
your Catholic childhood
speak to me.

I may leave our bed behind,
find my own, discover life's
missed presence is a cold night,
howling winds, a shaking
empty wall, or

I may stay here, in our bed,
sleep against the past, stretch
my arm to stroke the cat,
feel your presence, reach out,
encircle absence.

Porch Furniture

The year afterwards, I sprayed the wicker
        with white semi-gloss just because
it was time. Chips had formed, the former
        brightness faded and dull, and I
needed the comfort of the familiar.

I brought up pillows stored in the cellar
        through a long winter and laid them
around on the freshly painted furniture, gaining
        solace from their floral brightness.
The grill was another matter. Would it ignite?

Was there enough fuel to cook as I used to?
        flank steak marinated in soy sauce,
shrimp on metal skewers, done over gas heat,
        with oil, hoisin, and garlic.
I sit in a high-backed rocker, watch spirea

edge through the porch railing,
        think back to just a year ago when we
laughed with friends, smelled food, poured wine;
        I remember you still able to check the grill,
wonder, will I ever cook again?

Missing

Weeks, months, years later
I still wonder where you are.
I take off earrings just before bed,
brush my hair, unhook the old bra
with one snap missing, and feel you
hovering in the room
taking in the scene.

Sitting at a table for one,
I still wonder where you are.
Sometimes I count crumbs. Are
they all mine, or do I feel your
presence at my evening meal,
hear the clatter of an extra fork,
your silent sip of wine?

I look inside a book read twenty
years ago, and wonder where you are.
The story fits our time. We are real,
but not for long. You watch from
old pages, follow me with buried eye,
read print I cannot see. I feel your
touch, wonder where you are.

Meals of Memories

Imagine this! A wrinkled, aging critic,
cool, analytical, reliving youthful love affairs,
sumptuous meals, anxious now to lift the spoon—
place remembered taste against the tongue,
pleasuring both appetite and time.

I take a bite—see moonlight
covering newly blooming earth,
young bodies wrapped in ecstasy,
knowing morning will appear
all damp and cool with dew.

I see their youth press on, oblivious
of time, intense and hot as burning
mustard seeds against the tongue,
until worn out—passion spun,
they rise and turn to catch the light
of blinding noonday sun.

Fork touches plate, picks another bite—
real, savory, warm against the lips,
not chiseled from a frozen box
or dated with a stamp of faded blue.
I drool with joy. This taste of food
has brought me youth again!

I recognize the year, time of day, place,
the oval table, evening shadow lights,
all in a flash of scent and sight.
Smells drift back to take me in,
make real again those endless meals
I memorized with you.

Joyce Holmes McAllister's first poetry chapbook *Before We Knew* was published by Foot Hills Press in 2016. Within a little over a year, she published her second chapbook *Return*, put out by Yellow Sofa Press.

McAllister started writing poetry in secondary school. Her involvement with food and cooking also began when she was young, and developed over the years into a second passion, along with poetry. Besides cooking, she acquired a knowledge of food history as well as food literature, and became familiar with the personalities famous in that genre.

After her retirement as an administrator at Cornell University, she devoted much of her time to creative writing, primarily poetry. It was during this period that McAllister started writing poems about food, both humorous and serious. The collection *Food For Thought* is devoted to that effort.

CPSIA information can be obtained
at www.ICGtesting.com
Printed in the USA
BVHW050511021120
592165BV00001B/3